LIFE'S LITTLE LEAN ACCOUNTING INSTRUCTION BOOK

365 Days of Self Help for Lean-Thinking Accountants

By

BRIAN H. MASKELL
& SUSAN J. LILLY

BMA Inc.
100 Springdale Road Ste. 110
Cherry Hill NJ 08003 USA

information @maskell.com

Acknowledgements

We want to acknowledge the hard work of
all the accountants everywhere, working everyday
to shape and support their companies' lean journeys.

Hug a Controller – they deserve it !

1.
LEAN ACCOUNTING APPLIES LEAN THINKING TO ACCOUNTING, CONTROL, AND MEASUREMENT

2.
Waste is the enemy,
not the Accountant.
Put the Accountant on your side.

3.
Traditional accounting actively works against lean thinking.

4.
Lean Manufacturing can not be sustained long-term without Lean Accounting.

5.
Traditional accounting, control, and measurements systems are very wasteful.

6.
Traditional measurements motivate non-lean behavior.

7.
Strive for the two-transaction factory.
Receive Materials.
Ship products.
Nothing else needed.

8.
ALL TRANSACTIONS ARE WASTE.

9.
Learn to hate transactions.
Eliminate them ruthlessly.

10.
Transactions are to lean accounting
what inventory is to lean manufacturing.

11.
Lean Performance Measurements create control.
They work!
And people know what they mean.

12.
As your lean manufacturing processes become mature,
you need fewer transactions.

13.
Transactions provide <u>the illusion</u> of financial control
when operational processes are out-of-control.

14.
WHEN PROCESSES ARE IN CONTROL, TRANSACTIONS ARE NOT NEEDED.

15.
Lean Manufacturing brings operational processes under control.

16.

Standard Costing leads to bad decisions.
**Lean Accounting gives better
information.**
Better information gives better
decisions.

17.
BOX SCORE:
A 3-Dimensional View of the Value Stream

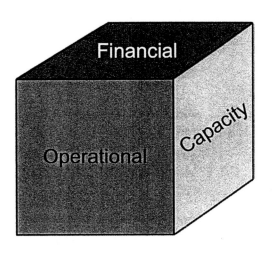

18.
BOX SCORE:
Are we making good use of our resources?
-Productive Capacity
-Non-productive Capacity
-Available Capacity

19.
Box Score:
Operational Measurements
Financial Results
Capacity Usage

20.

Box Score:
PERFORMANCE REPORTING
SEEING FINANCIAL BENEFITS
UNDERSTANDING STRATEGIC CHANGE
DECISION MAKING

21.

Box Score:

Caspian Company PA Motors Current		Current State	Make Product	Buy in China	Buy Locally
OPERATIONAL	Units per Person	29.31	26.05	32.56	32.56
	On-Time Shipment	97.2%	98.0%	95.7%	96.0%
	First Time Thru	54%	63%	52%	60%
	Dock-to-Dock Days	8.90	8.5	16.28	10.21
	Average Cost	$111.74	$113.10	$113.90	$112.66
	AP days - AR days	8.0	8.0	8.8	8.0
CAPACITY	Productive	31%	35%	31%	31%
	Non-Productive	56%	62%	56%	41%
	Available Capacity	13%	3%	13%	28%
FINANCIAL	Revenue	$1,611,456	$1,821,456	$1,821,456	$1,821,456
	Material Costs	$490,296	$586,296	$575,296	$672,296
	Conversion Costs	$497,933	$527,036	$545,933	$502,254
	Inventory	$221,163	$234,433	$448,961	$316,484
	Value Stream Profit	$623,226	$708,124	$700,226	$646,905
	Value Stream ROS	38.67%	38.88%	38.44%	35.52%
46.00%	Hurdle Rate	-7.33%	-7.12%	-7.56%	-10.48%

22.
Lean Performance Measurements create control.
They work!
And people know what they mean.

23.
Never jeopardize financial control!
Remove transactions <u>only</u> when the processes are
<u>proven </u>to be under control.

24.
Get out of the office. To the coal face!

25.
Walk the floor.
Go to the gemba.

26.
Get out of the office.
WORK TOGETHER.

27.
Transactions lead to reports and reports lead to *reconciliation's.*

28.
Transactions lead to reports and reports lead to *meetings.*

29.
MOST MEETINGS ARE WASTE.

30.
Most transactions have a reason.
Remove the reason;
remove the transaction.

31.
3-Way Match
is wallpapering over the cracks.
It masks problems but solves nothing.

32.
Every transaction is an opportunity for error.

33.
REVEAL MISTAKES.
DON'T FIX BLAME.
FIX PROBLEMS.

34.
Make waste visible.

35.
Be thankful for mistakes!
They offer opportunities to improve.

36.
STOP INSPECTING.
START PREVENTING.

37.
Ask the hardest questions, get the best answers.

38.
Ask: "What must be in place before we can safely remove these transactions."

39.
What must be in place in the value stream?
Consistent operational control.

40.
RUTHLESSLY ELIMINATE WASTEFUL TRANSACTIONS.

41.
60% done **now** is a good start.

42.
What can't be eliminated right now, simplify.

43.
Simplification and lean are synonyms.

44.
Simplify. Standardize. Automate.

45.
Eliminate the office.
Work together.

46.
Bar-coding an unneeded transaction is perfuming the pig.

47.
Get out of the office!
Meet around the boards.

48.
Manage by value stream.
Report by value stream.
Improve by value stream.
Plan by value stream.

49.
Bring the value stream team people together so
they work in one place.

50.
All reports are waste.

51.
**AUDITORS
GET YOUNGER EVERY YEAR.
LIVE WITH IT!**

52.
Balance measurements:
short term & long term.

53.
Link measurements to company strategy.
Use a Performance Measurements Linkage Chart

54.
Strategy leads to strategic measurements.
Strategic measurements lead to value stream measurements
Value stream measurements lead to cell or process measurements.

55.
Hourly measurements create control and keep you to takt time.

56.
Link all measurements to improvement cycles.

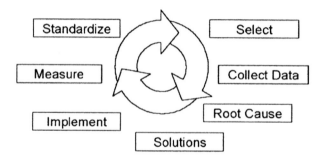

57.
Provide the information when it's needed.
Usually not monthly

58.
TIMELY INFORMATION:
RIGHT DATA,
RIGHT TIME,
RIGHT FORMAT.

59.
Motivate **only** lean behavior.

60.
Track outputs of processes, not inputs.

61.
Track exceptions.

62.
Don't track what went right.
Track what went wrong.

63.
Look for the holes,
not the donuts.

64.
A timely report is a pro-active report.

65.
Don't allocate non-value stream costs.
Show them **clearly.**

66.

**All value stream costs are direct costs.
Don't overcomplicate a simple situation.**

67.
Don't collect extra data for the accounting, control and
measurements systems.
If nobody else but you needs the data,
you might not need it either.

68.
Value Stream Costing.
Simple Summary Direct Costing of the Value Stream.

69.
Cost the value stream; not the product.
And certainly not the production job !!

70.
Value Stream Costing.

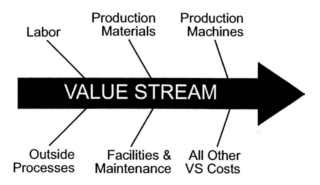

71.
Value Stream Costing.
All labor, machines, materials, outside processes, support
services, and facilities within the value stream.
Little or no allocation.

72.
Weekly value stream costs = Control of value stream costs

73.
Timely relevance triumphs over absolute accuracy.

74.
ONLY USE DATA OPERATIONS PEOPLE NEED FOR OTHER REASONS.

75.
Attention Accountants:
Join the value stream team.

76.
Attention Accountants:
Become a change agent.

77.
Attention Accountants:
Make reports plain and understandable to everyone.
Do it now!

78.
Attention Accountants:
No one understands absorption.

79.
Simple reports change the question …
from "What does this mean?"
to "What should we do?"

80.
**Can you control a production plant
using only non-financial reporting?**

81.
Again …
Can you control a production plant
using only one kind of transaction?

82.
"I would rather know today that it costs $100 than wait 6 weeks to know it costs $98.56324."

83.
Lean accounting systems
must be flexible.

84.
Lean accounting systems
must lend themselves to continuous simplification.

85.
**Lean Accounting systems
must themselves be lean.**

86.
Cost the Value Stream, not the product.

87.
All standard costs are wrong.

88.
Standard cost is a weapon
of mass production

89.

There is no such thing as a product cost.

90.

Repeat after me: "There is no such thing as a product cost".

91.

Product costs are not related to labor time.
Product costs are related to rate of flow.

92.
Product cost varies by flow rate, product mix, volume & by today's crisis.

93.
What is "margin?"

94.
Margins are fiction;
Because standard costs are wrong

95.
Basing decisions on standard cost leads to bad decisions.

96.
We don't need to know a product cost to make decisions.

97.
Price is driven by value.
Cost is driven by operational processes.
There is no relationship between price and cost.

98.
Make/Buy decisions:
How will this affect the value stream profit and
profitability? Never look at individual product costs.

99.
Quoting:
Price to the value you create for the customer.

100.
Capital Decisions:
Look at the impact on the value stream as a whole.
Use a Box Score.

101.
Low margin sales may be great business.
Don't believe the margins; they are misleading.

102.
Standard costs,
fully absorbed costs,
activity based costs,
RCA costs:
they are all product costs & they are all wrong.
They might be helpful in some places but not in lean.

103.
Cost information is so important to Lean.
You need much better ways to understand cost.

104.
Decisions MUST be made from the impact on Value Stream profitability.

105.
QUESTION: DO YOU HAVE A MENTAL MODEL?

106.
Answer: We all have *Mental Models.*

107.
We all look at things a little differently.

108.
What you see depends on where you stand.
So … go stand in the factory.

109.
Mental Models are our own frame of reference for
understanding what's going on around us.

110.
A *Mental Model* is much like a paradigm.

111.
Two groups can have quite different understandings
of the same situation
according to their viewpoints and assumptions.

112.
Traditional accountants and lean thinkers have
quite different *mental models*.

113.
Mental Models
are good things.

114.
Lean thinking views the world quite differently from traditional accounting & finance.

115.
Financial reports are useless if people can not immediately understand them.

116.
(Almost) nobody in your company understands the P&L

117.
No one uses variances.

118.
No one knows what Gross Profit means.
(Revenue minus COGS at standard cost)

119.
Put your financial reports into *plain English* so everyone can understand them.

120.
WHAT IS LEAN THINKING?

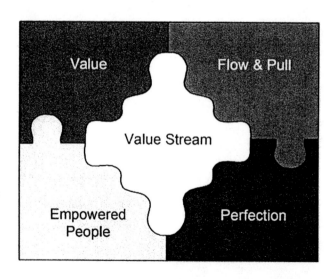

121.
Think by the *Five Principles of Lean Thinking*

122.
If it's not in line with the five principles of lean thinking, don't do it.

123.
**Lean thinking can not be sustained
long-term if Accounting & Finance
don't change.**

124.
Finance and accounting methods
are a manifestation of the company's culture.

125.
Empowered people
are accountable.

126.
Empowered people
have a formal and structured
improvement process.

127.
Lean thinking requires culture change.

128.
Traditional accounting *mental models* are not wrong.
They are based upon the assumptions of mass production.

129.
Traditional accounting methods
don't work for lean companies.

130.
Tried and true isn't necessarily true.

131.
Traditional accounting methods are non-lean
and encourage non-lean behavior.

132.
Value Stream =
The entire process for creating customer value.

133.
Value Streams

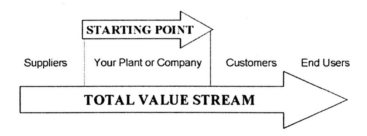

134.
Value streams extend outside the company to the suppliers- in one direction- and the customers in the other.

135.
Value comes when the flow of value-creating activities in the value stream is pulled by the customer.

136.
Waste starts when flow stops.

137.
WORK WITHOUT PULL IS WASTE.

138.
THREE KINDS OF FLOW:
1.MATERIAL FLOW
2.INFORMATION FLOW
3.CASH FLOW

139.
The *value stream* material flow starts with basic raw materials.

140.
The *value stream* stops with the ultimate disposal (or recycling)
of the product.

141.
Often more value is created by our services, attitude, culture,
and reputation than by the physical products.

142.
A product may be a commodity – a company never is.
Understand your value. Sell to your value.

143.
Value streams contain products, services and information.

144.
Order Fulfillment value streams start from sales and go through to cash collection.

145.
Product Development value streams start from product concepts and go through to launching the product.

146.
Not all activities
in the value stream create value.
Most are waste.

147.
We always recommend many days of expensive consulting.

148.
Lean organizations focus their attention around the perfection of the *value stream*.

149.
*Value stream maps
let you "see" the value stream.*

150.
Value stream **cost & capacity analysis
lets you "see" the financial impact
of lean improvements.**

151.
We must learn to see, and
learn to count.

152.
Don't view operations people as profligate
with accounting numbers.

153.
Don't work around; work with.
Don't work against; work with.

154.
Recognize that operations and finance
look from different perspectives.

155.
Everyone is responsible.
Everyone is on the team.
Power that is shared is empowering.

156.
Lean manufacturing people can not appreciate the assumptions
of traditional accounting. So they blame accountants.

157.
Traditional accounting methods are not
wrong. They are just wrong for lean.

158.
Traditional accounting reports invariably show
bad results when good lean things
are truly happening.

159.
Lean manufacturing people want to do the
right and lean things. They blame accountants
for misstating the obvious.

160.
COST = VALUE – REQUIRED PROFIT

161.
SIGNIFICANT INVENTORY REDUCTION NEGATIVELY AFFECTS PROFITABILITY.

162.
It bears repeating:
Lean accounting applies the assumptions of lean thinking
to accounting, control, and measurement.

163.
Lean Thinking has a habit of changing
<u>everything</u>. It's more like a marriage
than a one-night stand.

164.
Traditional systems record history.
They look backwards.

165.
**Driving is dangerous if you only look in
the rear-view mirror.**

166.
Lean accounting
predicts and affects the future.

167.
If you want to understand something,
go and see for yourself.

168.
The rate of change is getting
faster all the time.

169.
Some people are born for change;
some create their own change;
others have change thrust upon them.

170.
People usually resist change for good reasons.
Understand.
Address the reasons.

171.
Traditional accounting, control, and measurement systems are
complex and expensive.

172.
Departments wrong.
Value Streams right.

173.
Department reporting is **SO** non-lean!

174.
The Controller must maintain control. More so when
fundamental issues are changing. Lean brings control.

175.
Traditional accounting systems were developed by brilliant people between 1800 and 1925.

176.
All aspects of traditional accounting are important. But most are not required in lean companies.

177.
Progressio Quantocius [1]
(Make progress quickly.)

178.
60% is good enough.

179.
Don't dot every "i" and cross every "t."
Maintain control using lean methods.

180.
Do what you can.
Then do it again better.

181.
Lean change eliminates waste.
The waste becomes more capacity.

182.
Lean manufacturing is not for mass production.

183.
Mass production is moribund.

184.
Lean turns waste into available capacity.

185.
Traditional accounting, control and
measurement systems are full of waste.

186.
WHEN COMPANIES GO LEAN THEY
NEED LEAN ACCOUNTING METHODS.

187.

**Performance measurements
change behavior.**

188.
Right measurements linked to lean strategy
create success.

189.
All measurements must be visual.

190.
When it comes to measurements, less is more.

191.
Too many measurements will cloud the issue.

192.
**Always link your measurements
to your strategy.**

193.

Customer Value:
Why we are in business.

194.

Customers want to be treated individually.
Customers want long-term partnerships.

195.

Focus on customer value, not on cost.

196.
Customers pay for value.
Get good at making more value.

197.
Value stream cost analysis shows where cost is
expended within the value stream.

198.
Cost is <u>so important,</u>
you need much better information
than you get from a standard cost.
Value stream cost analysis gives that better information.

199.
Always take account of customer value when making decisions.
Target costing reveals customer value operationally.

200.
Customers value services as well as product features.

201.
Customer value partnership, innovation and reliability

202.
Quality Function Deployment (QFD)
identifies what customers value in
products and services.

203.
Understanding customer value is a complex blend
of products, process capability,
reputation & relationship.

204.
Focus groups & careful surveys create understanding of the
value proposition from the customer's viewpoint.

205.
Cooperate to create value.

206.
Show value information throughout the value stream.
Understand cost & understand value.

207.
Target costing links customer value to
product and service cost.

208.
Target costs are established for processes
as well as products.

209.
Value stream cost analysis
shows where cost is expended in the value stream.
Target costing
shows where value is created in the value stream.

210.
Match value creation and cost —
if you can.

211.
Customer value drives improvement
at every stage in the value stream.

212.
Customer value drives product design.

213.
Lean thinkers are from Mars;
traditional accountants
are from Venus.

214.

Traditional accountants measure direct labor costs because they assume direct labor is the most important conversion cost.
Lean thinkers disregard direct labor because it is just another fixed direct cost.

215.

Traditional accountants measure machine utilization because they assume profits come from full utilization of resources.
Lean thinkers disregard machine utilization because they want to make only what is needed today by the customer.

216.

There are no accounting variances in lean because there are no standard costs.

217.
Traditional accountants track cost variances as a method of maintaining control of expenditures.
Lean thinkers ignore cost variances because they control the business through controlling the processes.

218.
Traditional accountants believe all overheads need to be absorbed into product costs.
This is untrue.
Absorbtion hides waste and makes things complicated.

219.
Measuring earned value leads to people building inventory instead of waiting for customer pull.
Machine utilization metrics lead to overproduction.

220.
Purchase price variance (PPV)
leads to excess raw material inventory.

221.
Overhead absorption variance
makes people build too much product & inventory.

222.

Control the Value Stream, Control the Business.

224.
Understand capacity.

225.
Understand and evaluate available capacity.

226.
Traditional accounting systems maintain control by reporting huge numbers of historical transactions.
Lean accounting maintains control by understanding the causes of cost, performance and problems.

226.
Move from tracking history to understanding root cause and eliminating waste.

227.
If a single plant or location contained only one value stream;
then the costs would <u>all</u> be direct costs.
Think about it.

228.
Value stream costing is for managing the business;
NOT for reporting to corporate.

229.
Value stream management makes (almost) all cost direct.

230.
If all costs are direct, then cost and management accounting can be largely eliminated.

231.
Strive every day to simplify the operation and make costs direct.

232.
Sales, Operations, & Financial Planning (SOFP) is an excellent tool for planning production volumes and creating cooperation throughout the company.

233.
SOFP plans cover product families within value streams.

234.
SOFP addresses the company's
value-creating bottlenecks.

235.
SOFP plans what we sell, what we make,
and our cash flow.

236.
SOFP creates a jointly agreed "game plan".
Everyone works to plan.

237.
S&OP is used to create month-end information ahead of time.

238.
Lean Needs New Performance Measurements

239.
Most companies measure too much.
Most companies measure the wrong things.

240.
Never add performance measurements.
Replace old measurements with lean measurements.
Now!

241.
All the best things in life are hard to measure.

242.
Visual measurements only!
Don't hide information in the computers.

243.
You can't understand what you can't see.

244.
Measurements belong on visual boards.

245.
Visual boards lead to action and improvement.

246.
Visual boards disclose what must be done now.

247.
Visual boards: keep them simple.

248.
Visual boards: keep them current.

249.
Always date your visual boards.
A visual board without a date is a fossil.

250.
A hand-drawn chart today is worth two in the computer.

251.
Hand-drawn measures by the people using them
are effective for insight, change & problem solving.

252.
Focus measurements
on the right things.

253.
Create alignment throughout the organization using well designed measurements.

254.

The right measurements translate strategy into action.

255.
A few relevant measurements are worth 1000 analytical studies.

256.
Measurements must create continuous improvement.

257.
All measures must support the company's strategy.

258.
Measure production cells.
Measure non-production support processes.
Measure value streams.
Measure the company's strategic achievements.

259.
CELL MEASUREMENTS:
help the team get done today what needs to be done.

260.
CELL MEASUREMENTS:
make sure the cell is making to takt,
make sure the standardized work is working,
make sure the pull system is working.

261.
Typical cell measurements:
Day-by-the-Hour
WIP-to-SWIP inventory,
First-Time Through,
Operational Equipment Effectiveness.

262.
A day-by-the-hour chart keeps the cell to takt time.

263.
Tracking by the hour creates true control.

264.
WIP-to-SWIP tracks the pull system.

265.
First Time Through measures standardized work.

266.
Value stream measurements
drive continuous improvement.

267.
Continuous improvement empowers value stream teams.

268.
VALUE STREAM MEASURES:
show how much value we are creating,
if the processes are under control,
if material, information, & cash are flowing
if we are becoming better at what we do

269.
Typical value stream measurements:
Sales/person
Average product cost,
Dock-to-Dock,
AR days,
First time through

270.
Measurements tell us if our processes are under control.

271.
Most measurements are
visually displayed and manually created.

272.
Audit visual systems by watching.

273.
Financial measures are only used when a
common denominator is needed.

274.
Measurements will change over time.

275.
Measurement systems can vary from
one value stream to another.

276.
Add statistical analysis to
performance measurement.

277.
Move Quickly to Value Stream Management

278.
Value Stream Managers:
- -Grow the business
- -Create more value
- -Eliminate waste
- -Make tons of money

279.
Value stream managers have
full authority for the entire value stream.

280.
Key to lean: manage the business by value stream.

281.
Establish improvement cycles for the value stream.

282.
Move to summary direct costing of the value stream.

283.
Change the functional organization to a
value stream organization.

284.
Focus on customer value.

285.
Link statistical process control
to value stream improvement cycles.

286.
Establish the financial risk within the value stream and its processes.

287.
Lean eliminates waste.
The waste becomes available capacity.

288.
Use Value Stream Cost & Capacity Analysis to understand
capacity and how it changes.

289.
Use value stream cost management to pro-actively create
and deploy available capacity.

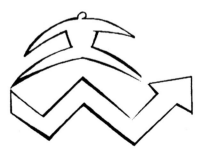

290.
If you have several people responsible for addressing
segments of the value stream, then no one is responsible
and accountable.

291.
Value streams are mini-entrepreneurial companies within the company.

292.
Most companies have no idea what their
products cost, but they have them to
5-decimal precision.

293.
Average value stream cost is a useful
performance measurement.

294.
*Most management decisions do not
require product cost.*

295.
Product cost varies according to the mix and volume of
products flowing through the value stream.

296.
Use value stream profitability to assess such things as:
1. make or buy,
2. quoting,
3. profitability,
4. product rationalization,
5. new product introduction.

297.
Value stream profitability shows what will really happen.
Using individual product costs do not.

298.
Prices should be set based upon value
from the point-of-view of the market or the customer.

299.
Don't allocate overheads.
Assign costs directly to the value stream.

300.
The primary determinant of cost is the cycle time through the value stream bottleneck work center.

301.
Costs are determined by how many of a product we can flow through the value stream.

302.
Understand the <u>features & characteristics</u> of the product and processes that drive the bottleneck cycle time … and therefore the cost.

303.
Use features & characteristics to link customer needs
to product features.

304.
If you need to calculate individual product costs,
use features & characteristics.

305.
If you can not calculate it with a spreadsheet,
it's too complicated.

306.
Work-in-Process Tracking...
who needs it?

307.
Reduce cycle time to eliminate the need for
work-in-process tracking.

308.
Eliminate job-step tracking in production.

309.
Eliminate backflushing by applying costs to the value stream directly and in summary.

310.
If you insist on backflushing – at least do it from shipment of the product. This keeps the transactions down to a minimum.

311.
Keep the bills of materials up-to-date and accurate.
Make the product/cell team responsible
for BOM accuracy.

312.
Flatten the bills.

313.
Eliminate production work orders.

314.
Track exceptions and post their costs.

315.
Eliminate standard costs & variance reporting.
Use summary direct costing.

316.
We hate inventory!
All inventories represent problems
we have not yet solved.

317.
Inventory: rats in the kitchen!

318.
Transactions are more rats in the kitchen.

319.
Inventory is the cost
of problems not yet resolved.
Transactions are the cost
of out-of-control processes.

320.
Warehouses are inventory hotels.
Stockrooms are inventory motels.

321.
Eliminate inventory
by removing the reasons why inventory is needed.
Remember: lean addresses root causes.

322.
Kanbans bring inventory under control
and ensure consistent inventory levels and value.

323.
Don't reduce inventory just to save money.
Eliminating waste reduces inventory.
Inventory is an <u>outcome</u> of lean improvement.

324.
Standard costs hide waste.
Make waste visible.
Eliminate standard costs.

325.
Eliminate annual physical inventory.
Move to cycle counting.

326.
Cycle counting is not used to make inventory accurate.
Use cycle counting to identify and eliminate
the causes of error.

327.
Then, eliminate cycle counting.

328.
The best way to resolve inventory accuracy problems
is to eliminate inventory.

329.
Stop tracking inventory on the computer;
as soon as your inventory is under control.

330.
As inventory is reduced, expense it.
Don't inventory it. Don't track it.

331.
If you have raw material inventory,
value it at average actual price,
or the blanket order price.

332.
Don't value WIP inventory.
Make it small & under control.

333.
If you have finished goods inventory,
value it by applying averages from the value stream costing.

334.

Paying Suppliers...
Introduce supplier certification.
Go to single sourcing.
Develop local suppliers.

335.
Use blanket purchase orders.
Negotiate products, price, & terms.
No delivery quantities or dates.

336.
Pay suppliers on monthly statements
rather than individual invoices.

337.
Use purchase credit cards for miscellaneous purchases.

338.
Voucher (or pay) on receipt.

339.
**Receiving Cash from Customers...
make it fast, make it simple.**

340.
Get blanket sales orders from customers.
Send invoices from the shipping area.
Fax, EDI or email sales invoices.
Stop printing paper copies!

341.
Use customer kanbans or call-off
instead of sales orders.

342.
Invoice by monthly statement.
Accept credit cards.
Allow the customer to work out the required payment.

343.
Eliminate accounts receivable by having
customers vouchers or pay on receipt.

344.
Budgets: Traditional accounting systems use budgets to create the illusion of control.
Detailed budgets do not create control.
Budgets create waste and manipulation.

345.
Lean companies create control by controlling the processes.

346.
If you must have budgets, budget monthly.

347.
If you must have budgets,
keep them to one total amount per cost center.
Empower the people to handle the details.

348.
Reduce the number of cost centers.
One to three cost centers per value stream.
Reduce the account codes included in the budgets.

349.
Budget by value stream.
Eliminate department budgeting.

350.
Integrate financial planning into the
monthly sales, operations, & financial planning
(SOFP). Get month-end results ahead of time.

351.
Think about General Ledger
and month-end in terms
of customer value.
What customer? What value?

352.
Financial accounting is almost totally regulated externally.
Regulated wasteful processes should be thoroughly
simplified then automated.

**353.
Computer systems are good at
standard, regulated processes.
Having people do standard,
regulated processes is a waste.**

354.
Study your bookkeeping processes.
Simplify, standardize, automate.

355.
Review the review and approval processes.
Eliminate reviews and approvals.

356.
Simplify & standardize the chart of accounts.

357.
Go to quarterly closes.

358.
Automate the month-end process.

359.
Look at shared services
to automate and cellularize the already
simplified and standardized processes.

360.
Automate the financial accounting processes.

361.
Leaders need their own standardized work.

362.
Consider outsourcing financial accounting.

363.
Become an agent of change
for your value stream.
Do some of the heavy lifting.

364.
Accounting must look for ways to help, not punish.

365.
Value is more important than cost.

366.
Lean improvements do not generally cut cost;
they create available capacity.
How you use the capacity
determines the financial <u>benefit</u> of lean.

367.
Listen up! This is important.
Lean enterprise is a long-term business growth program.
Traditional, short-term cost cutting does not work well with lean.

368.
Implement lean accounting through a well-developed maturity path.
As you mature with lean manufacturing
introduce more lean accounting.

369.
Changing accounting, control and measurement systems is difficult.
A step-by-step implementation plan is what it takes.

370.
Maintain control of the business through each step
of the maturity path.
As lean manufacturing brings the processes under control,
then you must simplify accounting methods.

371.
Every organization has a unique lean accounting maturity path;
including yours.

372.
Train the people in lean accounting concepts and methods.

373.
But remember, senior managers & executives do not need training.
They only require <u>briefing</u>.

374.
Typical accounting people spend 70% of their time in
bookkeeping activities, and less than 10%
on business improvement.
We must turn this around.

375.
Eliminate transactions and simplify processes.
Free up your time.
Use your time for lean improvement in the value stream.

376.
Live the five principles of lean thinking.
Understand lean manufacturing methods
better than the operational people.

377.
You are <u>not</u> the accountant on the team.
You are a team-member focused on creating
customer value, making continuous improvement
happen every week, and making more money.

378.
Become a change agent for proactive, radical
improvement of the value stream.
Do what it takes.
Push the operation further into lean.

379.
Get started.
Learn about Lean Accounting.

380.
60% is good enough.
Don't try to have all the problems solved
before you start.